KINGFISHER
RIDING CLUB
HORSE & PONY
BREEDS

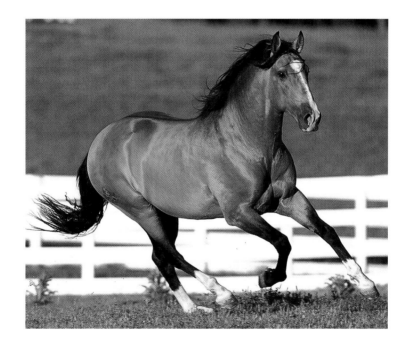

WRITTEN BY
Sandy Ransford

PHOTOGRAPHED BY
Bob Langrish

KINGFISHER
BOSTON

KINGFISHER

a Houghton Mifflin Company imprint
222 Berkeley Street
Boston, Massachusetts 02116
www.houghtonmifflinbooks.com

First published in 2003

10 9 8 7 6 5 4 3 2 1

1TR/0103/TWP/CLSN(CLSN)/150ENSOMA

LIBRARY OF CONGRESS CATALOGING-IN-
PUBLICATION DATA has been applied for.

ISBN 0-7534-5575-7

Designed and edited by:
Picthall & Gunzi Ltd.

Editor: Lauren Robertson
Designer: Dominic Zwemmer
DTP Assistant: Anthony Cutting
Editorial Assistant: Carmen Hansen
Editorial Director: Christiane Gunzi

Additional photography by:
Houghtons Horses p. 21br, p. 22b, p. 27tl,
p. 36bl, p. 40br, p. 44bl, p. 46br, p. 46bl,
p. 50bl, p. 51c, p. 59tr; Only Horses
Picture Library p. 26bl, p. 33b, p. 35bl,
p. 55b

For Kingfisher:
Editorial Director: Miranda Smith
Art Director: Mike Davis
DTP Manager: Nicky Studdart
DTP Coordinator: Primrose Burton
Consultant: Lesley Ward
Coordinating Editor: Stephanie Pliakas

Printed in Singapore

Contents

What is a breed?

Horses and ponies vary in shape and size. Some belong to a particular breed. This means that they share the same characteristics as other horses or ponies of the same breed. Horse breeds are divided into groups called coldblood, hotblood, and warmblood. The pony breeds are not usually classified in this way.

Coldbloods

Belgian Drafts (above) are typical coldblood horses. Coldbloods come from northern Europe, where the cool, damp weather produces plenty of rich grazing. This makes the horses bred there large and very strong.

Warmbloods

Warmblood breeds were produced by crossing hotbloods and coldbloods. This horse (left) is a warmblood, although it does not belong to a specific breed. It is a "type" called a heavyweight hunter. Types of horses are defined by the kind of work they do.

Hotbloods

The Anglo-Arab (above) is a fine example of the beauty, grace, and elegance of the hotblood breeds. Hotbloods originally came from the Middle East and North Africa, where poor grazing and the extreme climate produced a light, tough, fast horse.

Ponies

Ponies stand up to 14.2hh (57 in.), and most, like the Icelandics (right), are warmbloods. Ponies have shorter legs than horses, and they are stronger in relation to their size. They are sturdy, tough, and independent.

Types of horses

Horses and ponies vary in type from the large, heavily built, slow-moving draft horse to the slender, fast Thoroughbred; from the solid, weight-carrying cob to the elegant show pony. Types are usually a mixture of different breeds, although many are specially bred. For example, a heavy horse crossed with a Thoroughbred will produce a horse that is capable of carrying a large, heavy rider.

Driving types

Horses and ponies suitable for driving tend to have straight shoulders—on which the collar of the harness fits well—and upright pasterns. They often have high action, which looks good when they are pulling a carriage but would be very uncomfortable on a riding horse.

Heavy horses
This type of horse is massively built. Their bones are huge, and they have enormous muscles. They are capable of pulling very heavy weights.

Carriage horses
These types must also be strong, but they are lighter, more elegantly built, and often high-stepping. A matching pair is highly prized.

Riding types

A riding horse or pony has to be strong enough to carry its rider but narrow enough to ride. Sloping shoulders give a horse a long, low stride, which is comfortable for the rider. Sloping pasterns also make a horse a good ride, while powerful hindquarters and long hind legs give jumping ability.

Show pony
A show pony or horse has all the best points of a riding pony or horse. It must be beautiful, have good conformation and paces, and behave perfectly.

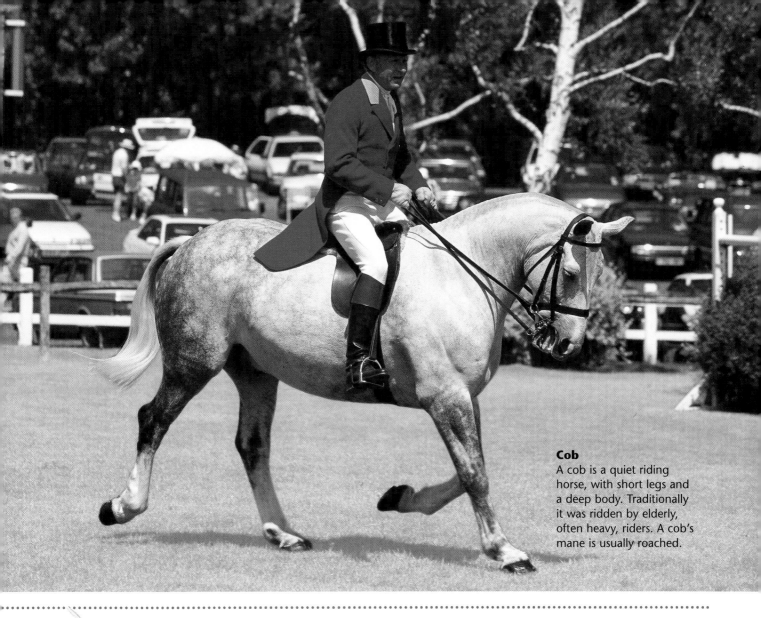

Cob
A cob is a quiet riding horse, with short legs and a deep body. Traditionally it was ridden by elderly, often heavy, riders. A cob's mane is usually roached.

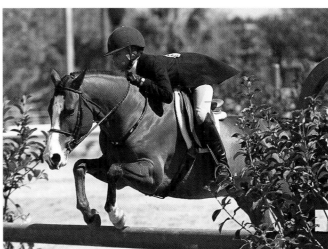

Polo ponies
These are actually small horses. They have to be fast, able to start, stop, and turn quickly, and must obey their rider's commands instantly.

Working hunter pony
This is more solidly built and plainer than the classic show pony. As well as being a good general riding pony, it must be able to gallop and jump.

Colors

The color of a horse's or pony's coat depends on the amount of pigment, or natural coloring, in its skin. Almost all horses and ponies have dark skin, except where they have white markings such as on the face and lower legs, where the skin is pink. Only rare, pure-white horses called albinos have pink skin all over. Most horses and ponies that we think are white are actually gray. They have dark skin, which you can see on their muzzles.

As horses age

As horses and ponies grow older their color may change. Grays are born dark and gradually become lighter, until they look white. Some grays develop dark, usually brown, flecks. This color is called "flea-bitten gray." Browns, blacks, bays, and chestnuts may have some white hairs in their coats, manes, and tails.

Bay is a rich, reddish-brown coat color with a black mane, tail, and lower legs.

Flea-bitten gray is a light gray color with dark, usually brown, flecks.

Bright bay is lighter than bay with more yellow in the coat color.

Brown is dark brown, often with paler areas. Also called dark bay.

Dapple gray has black and white hairs that form rings called dapples.

Black is black all over, including the mane and tail. Pure black is rare.

Eye color

The color of a horse's or pony's eyes, like that of its coat, is determined by the amount of pigment it has. As most horses and ponies have dark skin, most also have brown eyes. But occasionally, as with the albino and sometimes with spotted horses, the eyes are light-colored. In the Appaloosa breed the white of the eye can be seen all the time.

Brown eyes
The iris of the eye is dark brown. The white of the eye, which surrounds the iris, can be seen only when the horse is frightened or angry.

Wall eyes
In a "wall eye" the iris is bluish- or pinkish-white. This unusual color does not affect the horse's sight. These are also called china, blue, or glass eyes.

Hoof color

The color of the horn of a horse's or pony's hooves is related to the color of its coat on the leg just above the hoof. Black or dark-colored legs have dark hooves, which are called "blue." Where there are white socks or other leg markings the hooves are light-colored and are called "white." A horse may have hooves that are different colors.

Blue hoof and white hoof
The pony's leg shown on the left of the picture is dark and has a blue hoof. The leg on the right has a white sock, so the hoof is also white.

Striped hooves
Horse and pony breeds with spotted coats, such as the Appaloosa, have striped hooves (above). Light and dark stripes run up and down the feet.

Liver chestnut
is a darker chestnut, like the color of raw liver.

Chestnut
is red-gold or ginger, often with a darker or lighter mane and tail.

Blue roan
is black with white hairs through it, giving a bluish color.

Strawberry roan is chestnut with white hairs through it.

Yellow dun
is a yellowish, cookie-colored coat with black points.

Skewbald
is brown-and-white patches all over. Also called part-colored.

Piebald
is black-and-white patches all over. Also called part-colored.

Spotted is dark spots on a white coat or white spots on a dark coat.

Markings

The word "markings" means all the patches and stripes on a horse or pony that are a different color from its coat. These markings are usually white and appear on the face and legs. The shape and size of the markings varies a lot between different horses, and they are recorded and used to help identify the animal.

Face markings

Marks on the face are white and usually appear on the front of the face. These marks may cover a large area or a very small one and can be many different shapes. To make it easier to describe these marks and record them, different types of markings are given special names.

Blaze is a fairly broad white band down the face.

Blaze

Flesh marks

Stocking

Flesh marks

White patches on the underside of a horse's belly and on its flanks are called "flesh marks." These marks are often seen on Clydesdale horses (left). Sometimes horses have white marks on their backs or in other places. These are usually the result of an injury or wound and are called "acquired marks."

Leg markings

Leg markings are mostly white and are usually called "socks" or "stockings," but there may also be dark marks. When markings are written down to help identify a horse, they are described very carefully. For example, a certificate may say "white midpastern to coronet" or "white to midcannon."

Socks are white marks that go above the fetlock but not as far as the knee or hock.

Stockings are white marks that reach and sometimes cover the knee or hock.

Stripe is a narrow band of white down the face.

Star is a white mark of any shape on the forehead.

Snip is a patch of white on the nose between the nostrils.

Whorl is a ring of hair that grows in different directions.

Eel stripe

Primitive breeds, such as Przewalski's Horse (right) and Fjord and Highland ponies, often have a black stripe running along their backs from the mane to the tail. This is called an "eel" or "dorsal" stripe and is usually seen with a dun-colored coat.

Eel stripe

Bald face

A very broad white blaze that goes all the way across the front of a horse's face is called a "bald face." It reaches as far as the eyes and covers the horse's muzzle.

White coronets cover the area just above the hoof, which is called the coronet.

White pasterns cover the pastern area between the hoof and the fetlock joint.

Ermine marks are small, dark spots on white socks next to dark marks on the hooves.

Zebra marks are horizontal dark stripes on the lower legs seen in ancient breeds.

Hotblood
Horses

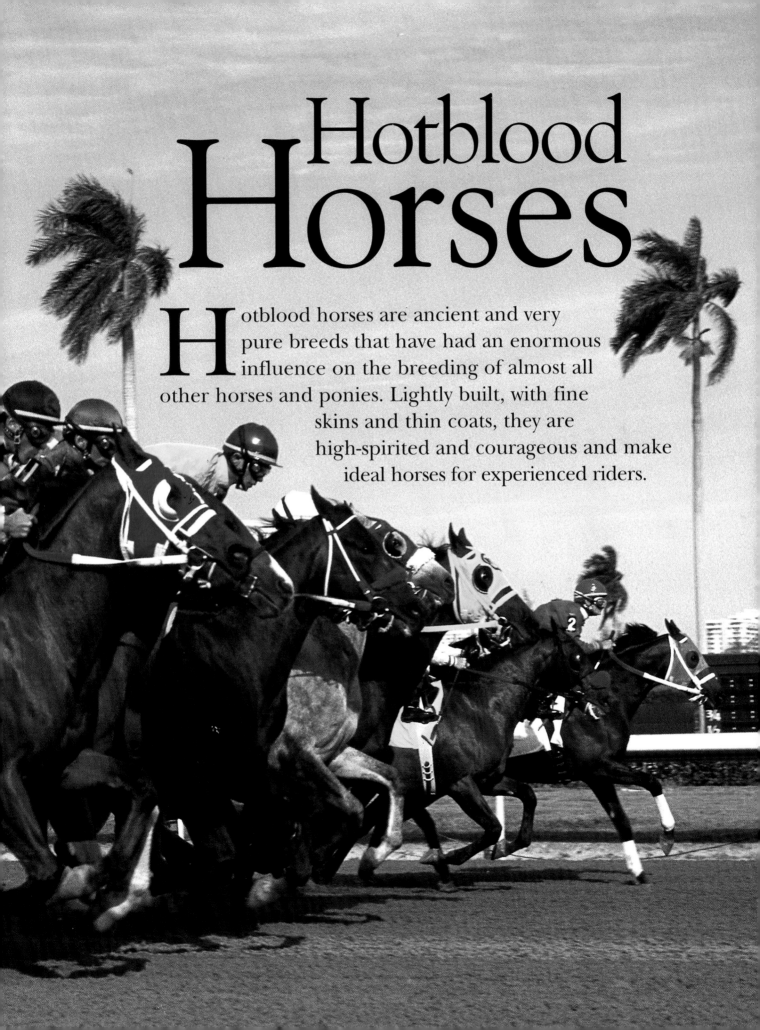

Hotblood horses are ancient and very pure breeds that have had an enormous influence on the breeding of almost all other horses and ponies. Lightly built, with fine skins and thin coats, they are high-spirited and courageous and make ideal horses for experienced riders.

Arabian

The Arabian is probably the oldest and most beautiful breed of horse in the world. It has played an important part in the development of horse and pony breeds in almost every country. With its high head and tail carriage, great presence, and floating action, an Arabian horse is instantly recognizable. Although it is a small horse, the Arabian is strong and is famous for its stamina.

Arabian head

The head is small and elegant, with a "dished," or concave, profile. The neck has a high crest. The angle at which the neck joins the head, called the mitbah, is seen only in this breed.

An Arabian's back is short and compact because it has fewer bones in its spine than other horses. The joints of the legs are flat, and the pasterns are sloping. The chest is broad, and the feet are hard and well-formed.

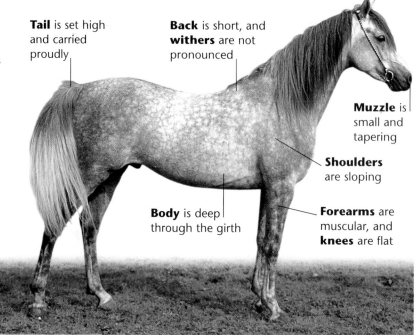

Tail is set high and carried proudly

Back is short, and **withers** are not pronounced

Muzzle is small and tapering

Shoulders are sloping

Body is deep through the girth

Forearms are muscular, and **knees** are flat

Mare and foal
An Arabian horse is high-spirited and courageous, but it also has a kind and gentle nature, making it easy to handle. Arabian foals are lively and inquisitive.

Desert horses

Arabians were first bred in the deserts of the Arabian peninsula, where they have existed for at least 4,000 years. Poor food and harsh conditions have produced a small, fast horse that is strong and tough. Arabians are raced over more than 280 mi. (150km) and are regarded as prized possessions by their owners.

Key facts

- **Place of origin**
  The Arabian peninsula,
  now called Saudi Arabia

- **Height**
  14.2–15hh (57–59 in.)
  or larger

- **Color**
  Mostly chestnut, bay,
  and gray; brown and
  black are seen rarely

- **Uses**
  General riding;
  showing; endurance riding;
  specialist racing; also as
  a cross with other breeds
  to produce quality show
  horses and ponies

- **Characteristics**
  Courageous and gentle

Thoroughbred

The Thoroughbred is the fastest breed of horse in the world. It was produced in England in the 1600s and 1700s by crossing three Arabian stallions—the Darley Arabian, the Godolphin Arabian, and the Byerley Turk—with English mares. Thoroughbreds have developed into perfect racehorses. They have also had a huge effect on horse breeding throughout the world. They succeed at all types of equestrian sports and make good riding horses.

Thoroughbred breeding

Thoroughbred horses are very valuable. Those to be used for racing are called bloodstock and are bred from former racehorses on special stud farms. Young horses are turned out together in paddocks until they are old enough to begin their training.

On the gallops

When Thoroughbred racehorses have become used to carrying a rider and obeying commands, they are trained on stretches of land called gallops. Here they can gallop for long distances. They usually exercise in groups, called strings, supervised by their trainers.

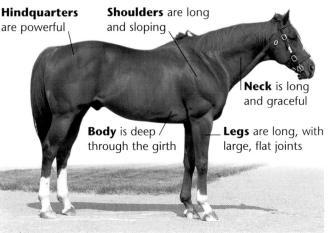

Hindquarters are powerful

Shoulders are long and sloping

Neck is long and graceful

Body is deep through the girth

Legs are long, with large, flat joints

Steeplechasing

Thoroughbreds compete in both flat racing and racing over fences, which is called steeplechasing. The gray horse above right is Desert Orchid, one of the most successful recent steeplechasers. He is shown here racing in Cheltenham, England, in 1990.

Eventing
Many horses that compete in eventing are either pure- or partbred Thoroughbreds.

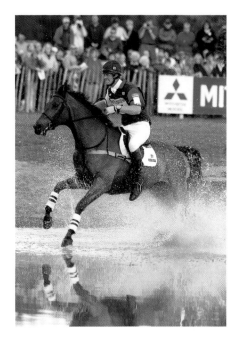

Many people believe that this breed is the perfect riding horse. Its sloping shoulders and long pasterns produce long, low strides, making it comfortable to ride. Its powerful quarters give it great speed. It is light and graceful, yet strong, and has great stamina.

Key facts

- **Place of origin**
  England

- **Height**
  15.2–16.2hh
  (61–66 in.)

- **Color**
  Brown, bay, black, chestnut, gray; always solid colors

- **Uses**
  Racing; riding; showing; dressage; show jumping; eventing

- **Characteristics**
  Fast and courageous but also highly strung and sometimes difficult to handle

Anglo-Arab

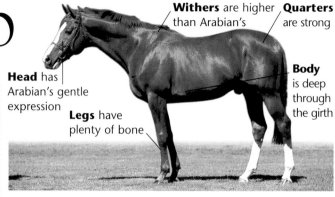

Withers are higher than Arabian's

Quarters are strong

Head has Arabian's gentle expression

Legs have plenty of bone

Body is deep through the girth

The Anglo-Arab is a cross between the Arabian and the Thoroughbred. It has the beauty and intelligence of the Arabian and the size and speed of the Thoroughbred. Although the breed originated in England, much of its development took place in France.

Endurance riding

Anglo-Arabs, as well as purebred and partbred Arabians, compete very successfully in long-distance endurance rides. The horses must be extremely fit and have great stamina because they may have to travel up to 50 mi. (80km) per day at an average speed of 9 mph (14–15km/h). Some endurance rides last for more than one day.

Its head is straighter in profile than the Arabian's, and the horse looks more like a Thoroughbred because of its greater size. Its long legs enable it to move with great speed. Its size means that it does very well in eventing and show jumping, as well as in dressage.

Key facts

- **Height**
  15.2–16.2hh
  (61–66 in.)

- **Color**
  Bay, chestnut, brown, gray

- **Uses**
  Riding; endurance; dressage; show jumping

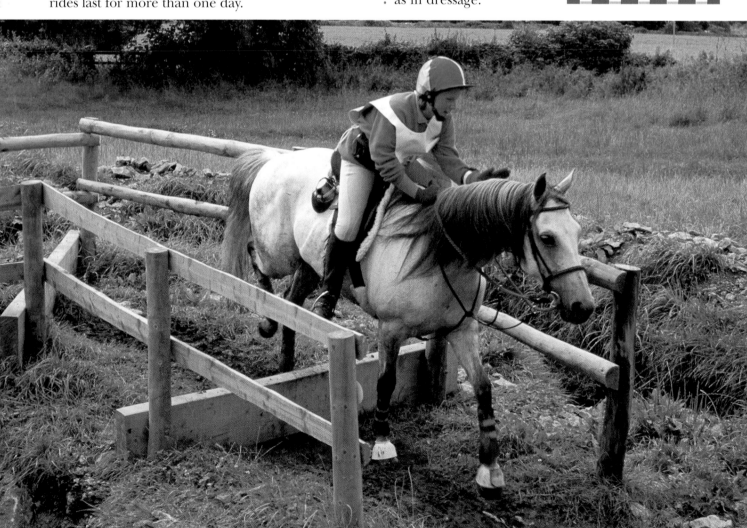

Barb

The Barb comes from Morocco, in North Africa, and is one of the world's oldest breeds. Although it is not beautiful, the Barb is sound and tough and has great stamina. It is capable of great speed over short distances.

Mane and **tail** are thick and full

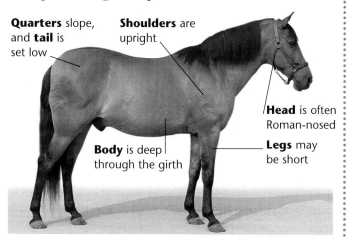

Quarters slope, and **tail** is set low

Shoulders are upright

Head is often Roman-nosed

Body is deep through the girth

Legs may be short

Head shape

The Barb is such an ancient breed that its skull shape is similar to that of primitive horses. Its head is quite large and plain and does not have the Arabian's grace and beauty.

The Barb, like the Arabian, has had a great influence on horse breeding throughout the world. The Spanish Horse, from which many horse and pony breeds were developed, was itself descended from the Barb. The breed is the traditional mount of the Berbers of North Africa.

Akhal-Teke

Bred in the deserts of Turkmenistan, north of Iran, the Akhal-Teke is an unusual-looking horse. It has a long, lean body and neck and long legs. It is capable of great feats of endurance and is used for long-distance riding, racing, jumping, and dressage.

The Akhal-Teke has been bred for thousands of years. It is spirited and courageous, hardy and strong. This breed stands around 15.2hh (61 in.) and has a fine coat and a silky mane and tail. The most prized color is this unique metallic golden dun.

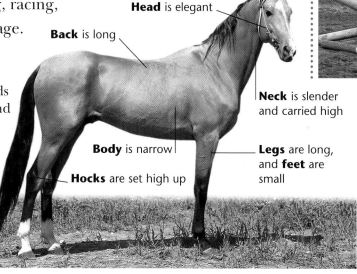

Head is elegant

Back is long

Neck is slender and carried high

Body is narrow

Legs are long, and **feet** are small

Hocks are set high up

Good jumper

Because of its great stamina, the Akhal-Teke is mainly known for its success in long-distance riding and racing. But it is also a good jumper and competes successfully in both show jumping and dressage.

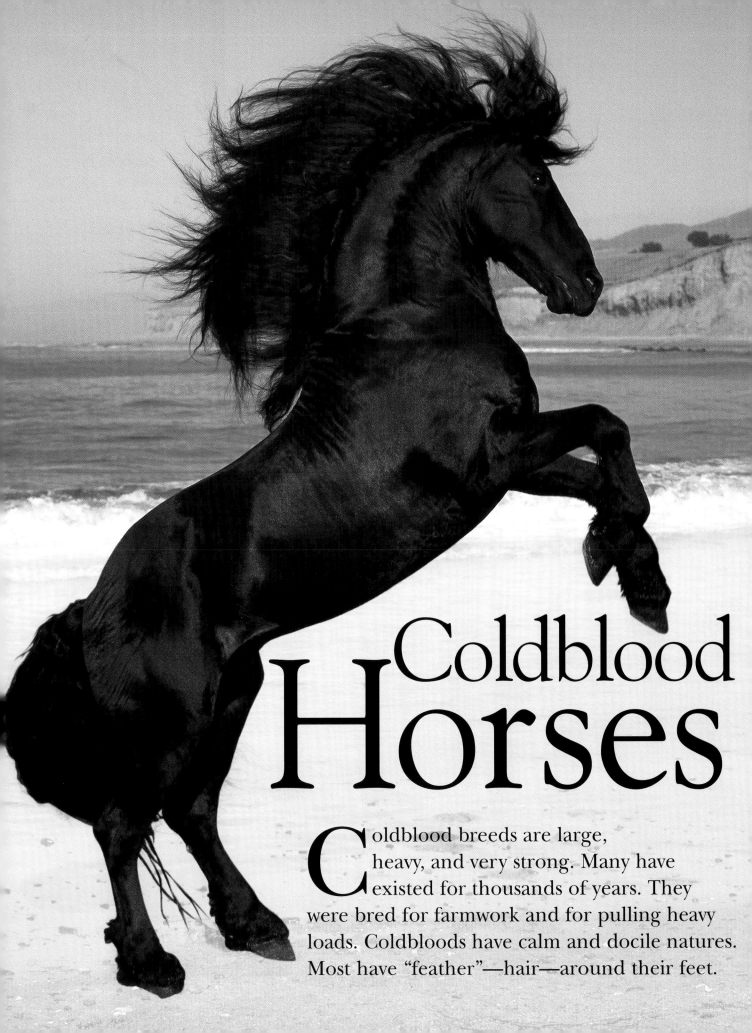

Coldblood
Horses

Coldblood breeds are large, heavy, and very strong. Many have existed for thousands of years. They were bred for farmwork and for pulling heavy loads. Coldbloods have calm and docile natures. Most have "feather"—hair—around their feet.

Ardennais

This heavy draft horse has been bred in the Ardennes region, on the borders of France and Belgium, for hundreds of years. It is probably descended from medieval warhorses. In the 1800s the Ardennais developed into two main types—a massive farm horse and a more lightweight animal.

Neck is heavily crested

Hindquarters are powerful

Head is broad

Legs are short and muscular

Body is compact

Crowd pullers

Ardennais are not often used for farming today, but these good-natured, easy-to-handle horses are still popular at shows. This pair, pulling a farm wagon, are the typical red roan color.

Ardennais stand between 15 and 16hh (59–64 in.). They are tough, hardy animals and are able to withstand a harsh climate and survive on poor food. Ardennais horses are often roan in color, although they may also be bay, chestnut, or gray.

Hindquarters are very muscular

Neck has a large crest and a fine, silky mane

Head is elegant

Shoulders are powerful

Legs are huge and carry little feather

Boulonnais

The Boulonnais comes from the area around Boulogne in northeast France. Two types of Boulonnais were bred—one was a heavy farm worker, and the other was a lighter, faster horse called a *mareyeur* (meaning "fish seller"). This horse was used for transporting fish from the coast to Paris.

Despite its size, the Boulonnais is an elegant horse owing to its Arabian and Barb ancestors. It is usually gray but is also sometimes black, roan, bay, or chestnut. This horse is well-proportioned and has a fine coat and thick, silky mane and tail hair. It stands between 16 and 17hh (64–68 in.).

Fast action

The Boulonnais can move faster than most heavy horses and has lower knee action. Some still work on farms, but to ensure the breed does not die out, the French government breeds Boulonnais.

Percheron

This powerful breed comes from La Perche in northern France. Its ancestors carried knights who wore heavy armor. In the 1700s the Percheron was crossed with the Arabian, giving it greater quality and better action. These horses are clean-legged, a great advantage when they work on the land.

Quarters slope steeply from croup

Shoulders are sloping

Forehead is broad

Body is deep through the girth

Legs are short and very strong

Key facts

- **Place of origin**
  Normandy, France
- **Height**
  16.1–17.2hh (64–69 in.)
- **Color**
  Gray or black
- **Uses**
  Farmwork; driving

One of the tallest horses that has ever lived was a Percheron. It stood 21hh (83 in.), though not many of them are as large as that. Percherons are broad, compact, and very strong, with sturdy legs and good feet. The breed has a more elegant appearance, lower action, and a finer head than most heavy breeds because of its Arabian blood.

Carriage horses
Although some Percherons still work on the land, they are also popular as carriage horses. Despite being so large, they have a low, free action and move easily. They are docile and work well.

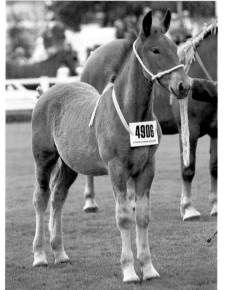

Suffolk foal
Suffolks mature early and live for a long time. This foal may start its working life at two years old and continue for many years. Suffolks are valuable as both farm horses and draft horses in towns.

Suffolk

Often called the Suffolk Punch, this is the most purebred of all of Great Britain's heavy horses. All Suffolks are descended from one stallion called the Horse of Ufford, which was born in 1768. The Suffolk is stocky, with short legs, and is always chestnut in color. Some Suffolks are used for farmwork, but the breed is now mostly seen in the showring.

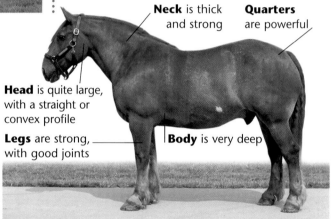

Neck is thick and strong

Quarters are powerful

Head is quite large, with a straight or convex profile

Legs are strong, with good joints

Body is very deep

The Suffolk has a round, barrel-shaped body on short, strong legs. Its chest is wide, and it has a thick neck with low withers. Despite its bulk, the horse moves freely and has an energetic trot. It has a friendly and docile temperament and is easy to handle.

Key facts

- **Place of origin**
  Suffolk, England

- **Height**
  16–16.3hh
  (64–66 in.)

- **Color**
  Always chestnut, with no white markings except on the face

Farm horse

The Suffolk was bred to work on farms in eastern England. The lack of feather on its legs is an advantage, as it means that the heavy clay soil does not cling to them. Suffolks do not need a lot of food, which makes them inexpensive to keep.

Shire

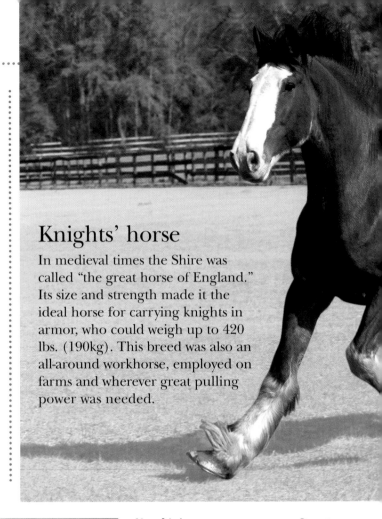

Tall and extremely strong, the Shire is probably the heaviest of England's heavy horses. It can weigh up to 2,700 lbs. and may stand up to 17.2hh (69 in.). Its girth can measure up to 8 ft. The Shire gets its name from the English counties where it was bred (Derbyshire, Staffordshire, Lincolnshire, and Leicestershire). Shire horses often worked on farms. Many brewers also used them to pull carts called drays to deliver beer in cities.

Knights' horse

In medieval times the Shire was called "the great horse of England." Its size and strength made it the ideal horse for carrying knights in armor, who could weigh up to 420 lbs. (190kg). This breed was also an all-around workhorse, employed on farms and wherever great pulling power was needed.

Plowing match

There are not many working Shire horses today, but they are often seen at plowing matches and shows. Their manes are braided with ribbons, and their bridles and harnesses gleam with polished brass. They are a magnificent sight, and their strength and gentleness are much admired.

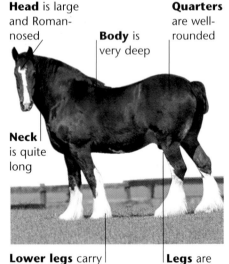

Head is large and Roman-nosed

Body is very deep

Quarters are well-rounded

Neck is quite long

Lower legs carry a lot of feather

Legs are very strong

This tall and extremely powerful horse is able to pull five times its own weight. A Shire is usually black, bay, brown, or gray in color. Its legs often have long white stockings, and the feather is fine and silky. Shires' tails are often cut short, which means that they lose their natural flyswatters.

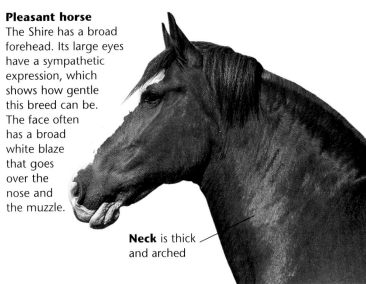

Pleasant horse
The Shire has a broad forehead. Its large eyes have a sympathetic expression, which shows how gentle this breed can be. The face often has a broad white blaze that goes over the nose and the muzzle.

Neck is thick and arched

Key facts

- **Place of origin**
  The Midlands, in England
- **Height**
  16.2–17.2hh (66–69 in.)
- **Color**
  Bay, brown, black, or gray
- **Uses**
  As dray horses; for showing

Clydesdale

The Clydesdale is related to the Shire but is lighter in build. This breed comes from Scotland, where it was originally used for farmwork. Later it was used to pull various forms of transportation, including coal wagons. Today the Clydesdale is seen at shows and in plowing matches. It is also crossed with Thoroughbreds to produce heavyweight riding horses.

Clydesdales are usually bay, brown, black, or roan. They often have white markings that start at their feet and go right up the legs. Some cover part of the horse's belly, and the face may be mostly white too. These big horses stand around 16.2 to 17hh (66–67 in.).

Back is short and strong

Withers are higher than the croup

Profile is straighter than a Shire's

Body is deep through the girth

Legs are powerful

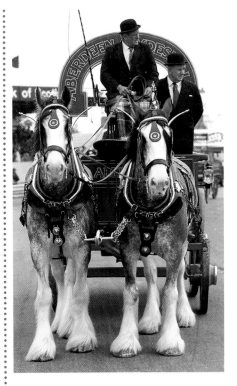

Trade turnout
Beautifully decorated Clydesdales are often seen at shows, harnessed to brightly painted vehicles called trade turnouts.

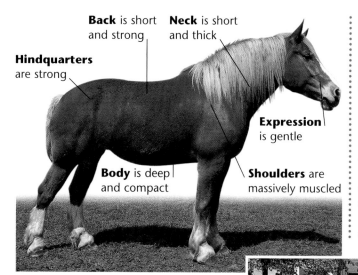

Back is short and strong

Neck is short and thick

Hindquarters are strong

Expression is gentle

Body is deep and compact

Shoulders are massively muscled

Belgian Draft

This ancient breed dates back to Roman times and is also known as the Brabant and Brabançon. The Belgian Draft's ancestors were warhorses, and they helped create the Shire, Clydesdale, and possibly the Suffolk. The breeding of Belgian Drafts was carefully controlled to produce an impressive horse.

Standing 16 to 17hh (64–68 in.), the Belgian Draft is a compact, very strong horse. It is usually chestnut or red roan in color. This breed of horse is good-natured and intelligent. It is a popular breed in the United States, as well as in its native Belgium.

Still working

Today the Belgian Draft is not used much for farmwork, but it can still be seen working in harness. This pair is pulling a trolley through the streets of a small, European-style town in California.

Noriker

This Austrian breed dates back to the 1500s. Its name comes from the word "Noricum," which was a Roman province situated where Austria is now. The Noriker is related to the Haflinger and was bred to work on the farms and forests of the Austrian Alps. It is strong, hardworking, and easy to handle.

Mane and **tail** are often flaxen

Back is long

Nostrils are wide

Legs are strong and carry little feather

Girth is huge

Broad horse

The Noriker has a broad chest, and its girth measurement should not be less than 60 percent of its height. It has short, sturdy legs. This breed's tough constitution helps it withstand the harsh Alpine winters.

The Noriker stands between 16 and 17hh (64–67 in.) and is chestnut, brown, or black in color. Its legs are strong, and its action is longer and lower than that of many heavy breeds. It has a calm temperament, is surefooted, and is economical to keep.

Friesian

This attractive breed from the Netherlands was the mount of German and Friesian knights during the Crusades. It was used for farmwork and, in the 1800s, for trotting races. Friesians are still ridden, but they are used mostly as carriage horses. As they are black, they are often used for funerals.

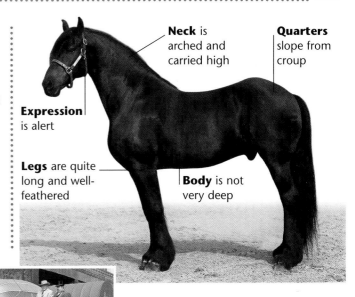

Neck is arched and carried high

Quarters slope from croup

Expression is alert

Legs are quite long and well-feathered

Body is not very deep

Four-in-hand

Friesians are popular driving horses. They are very handsome, and they have a fast, high-stepping trot. This team, called a four-in-hand, is owned by Harrods, a famous department store in London, England.

Standing between 15 and 16hh (59–64 in.), the Friesian is black all over, though some may have a small white star on their foreheads. The horse is lighter in build than many heavy breeds. The Friesian has a good temperament and is easy to handle.

Neck is short and huge

Quarters slope steeply from the croup

Legs have huge muscles

Head has a straight profile

Legs carry a lot of feather

Shoulders are muscular

Dutch Draught

This breed is believed to be the most massively built of all European heavy draft horses. It was developed in the late 1800s and early 1900s from the Ardennais and native horses. The Royal Dutch Draught Horse Society controls its breeding. The result is a very heavy and powerful working horse.

The Dutch Draught stands around 16.3hh (66 in.) and is usually chestnut, bay, roan, gray, or black in color. Although it is very heavy, its action is free and active. This breed matures early and is long-lived. The Dutch Draught has a quiet nature and is a good worker.

Show horse

Today, Dutch Draughts are mostly seen in the showring, where they may drive a variety of carts. Some, however, are still used to pull vehicles around city streets, selling or advertising goods.

Warmblood Horses

Most of the horse and pony breeds throughout the world are classed as warmbloods. Many types of horses and ponies also belong to this group. Warmblood horses include the highly successful German and Dutch competition horses and most of the American breeds.

Swedish Warmblood

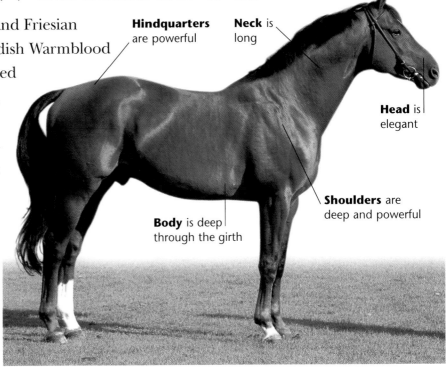

Bred from Spanish, oriental, and Friesian horses in the 1600s, the Swedish Warmblood was a cavalry horse. Later the breed was crossed with Thoroughbreds, Trakehners, Hanoverians, and Arabians. Today it is a competition horse—its is good at jumping, eventing, and dressage.

Standing around 16.2 to 17hh (66–68 in.), the Swedish Warmblood is a big, athletic horse. It has powerful shoulders and quarters, strong legs, and good feet. Its calm temperament and sensible attitude help make it good at dressage. It can be any solid color.

Hindquarters are powerful

Neck is long

Head is elegant

Shoulders are deep and powerful

Body is deep through the girth

Selle Français

The Selle Français (meaning "French saddle") was bred in Normandy, France, in the 1800s from native Norman horses and imported English Thoroughbreds. In the middle of the 1900s French Trotters, Thoroughbreds, Arabians, and Anglo-Arabs were used to develop the breed.

The Selle Français is a well-built horse, with strong legs and lots of muscle. Its body is quite long, and its withers are high. It stands around 16hh (64 in.). It is intelligent, with a calm temperament, and is agile and athletic. It may be any solid color.

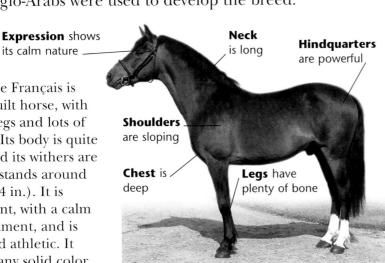

Expression shows its calm nature

Neck is long

Hindquarters are powerful

Shoulders are sloping

Chest is deep

Legs have plenty of bone

Good jumper

This horse excels at show jumping and eventing. It tackles difficult cross-country fences bravely and is good at dressage. It makes a good all-around riding horse. In France some Selle Français are bred especially for racing.

Competition breeds

Although many breeds and types of horses are good at dressage, eventing, and show jumping, the breeds described here are particularly well-known for this. They were produced by crossing farm and carriage horses with English Thoroughbreds. This made lighter, faster horses, while keeping the calmer nature of the heavier animals.

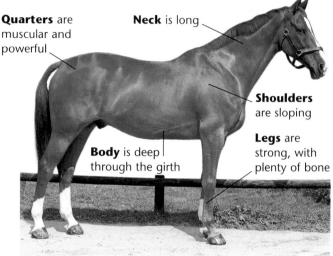

Quarters are muscular and powerful

Neck is long

Shoulders are sloping

Body is deep through the girth

Legs are strong, with plenty of bone

Dutch Warmblood

This breed was created in the 1900s by crossing the Gelderlander and the Groningen with the English Thoroughbred. It is possibly the most successful of the competition breeds. These horses are strong and athletic, with a calm temperament.

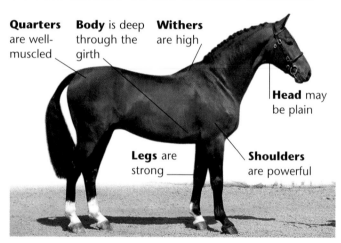

Quarters are well-muscled

Body is deep through the girth

Withers are high

Head may be plain

Legs are strong

Shoulders are powerful

Hanoverian

This breed was developed in the 1700s by crossing Holsteiners with local mares. This produced a strong horse that was used for farmwork. Trakehners and English Thoroughbreds were used to improve the breed and create a first-class competition horse.

Dressage champion
Strong, athletic, and with good action, this breed is superb at dressage. This picture shows Isabell Werth on Gigolo riding for Germany.

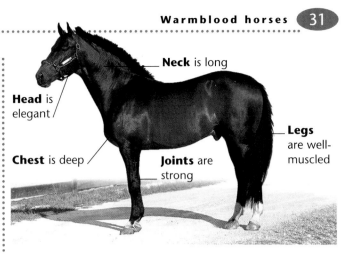

Neck is long

Head is elegant

Chest is deep

Joints are strong

Legs are well-muscled

Famous partnership
One of the most famous dressage partnerships of all time was Jennie Loriston-Clarke and Dutch Courage, here giving a demonstration of long-reining.

Holsteiner

Between the 1600s and 1800s Holsteiners were used as carriage horses. Since the 1800s they have been bred for riding. They are excellent at cross-country jumping and do well in dressage and show jumping.

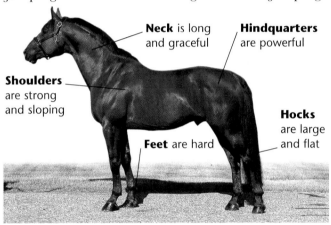

Neck is long and graceful

Hindquarters are powerful

Shoulders are strong and sloping

Feet are hard

Hocks are large and flat

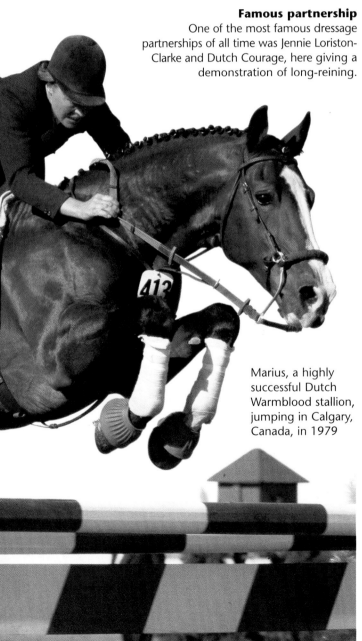

Marius, a highly successful Dutch Warmblood stallion, jumping in Calgary, Canada, in 1979

Trakehner

This breed began in East Prussia in the 1200s. Originally a carriage horse, it was crossed with Arabians and Thoroughbreds to produce cavalry horses. It is a first-class dressage, jumping, and eventing competitor.

Key facts

Dutch Warmblood
- **Height**
  15.3–16.3hh (62–66 in.)
- **Color**
  Any solid color

Hanoverian
- **Height**
  16–17hh (64–68 in.)
- **Color**
  Any solid color

Holsteiner
- **Height**
  16–17hh (64–68 in.)
- **Color**
  Any solid color

Trakehner
- **Height**
  16–17.2hh (64–69 in.)
- **Color**
  Any solid color

Oldenburg

The tallest and heaviest of the German warmblood breeds, the Oldenburg was bred in the 1600s as a coach horse. It was named after the area of Germany from which it came and the man who bred it, Count Anton von Oldenburg. Its ancestors include Friesian, Neapolitan, Spanish, Cleveland Bay, English Thoroughbred, and Norfolk Roadster horses. Today it is used for driving, dressage, and show jumping.

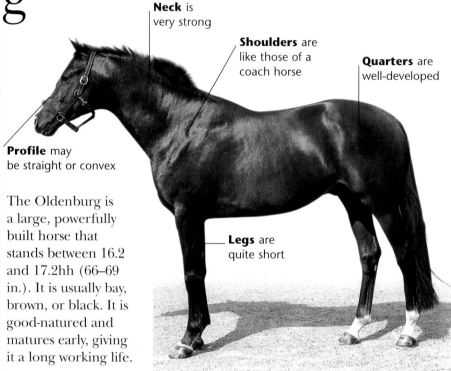

Neck is very strong

Shoulders are like those of a coach horse

Quarters are well-developed

Profile may be straight or convex

Legs are quite short

The Oldenburg is a large, powerfully built horse that stands between 16.2 and 17.2hh (66–69 in.). It is usually bay, brown, or black. It is good-natured and matures early, giving it a long working life.

Gelderlander

This breed comes from the Gelder area of the Netherlands, where it has been bred since the 1800s. Gelderlanders were then used mainly as carriage horses, but they were also expected to do light farmwork and double as riding horses. Their ancestors include the Oldenburg and the Thoroughbred.

The heavily built Gelderlander stands 15.2 to 16.2hh (61–66 in.) and is usually chestnut in color. It often has a wide white blaze on its face and white stockings on its legs. Although it is not thought of as a beautiful horse, it is very strong. The Gelderlander has a gentle, docile temperament, making it easy to handle.

Tail is set high

Shoulders are upright

Head is large and plain

Legs are strong

Carriage horses

Although Gelderlanders are no longer used for farmwork, they are still popular carriage horses and are used in driving competitions. They are also useful heavyweight riding horses, due to their size and strong build. These horses are not fast, but they are good jumpers.

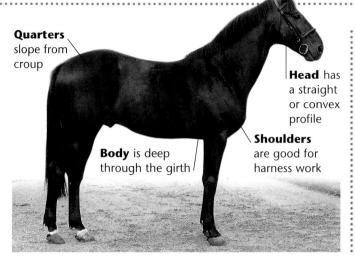

Quarters slope from croup

Head has a straight or convex profile

Body is deep through the girth

Shoulders are good for harness work

French Trotter

This breed was developed in Normandy, France, in the 1800s to compete in the new sport of trotting. The first trotting racecourse in France opened in Cherbourg in 1836. The French Trotter's ancestors are the Norfolk Trotter, the English Thoroughbred, and horses from the Normandy region.

The French Trotter stands around 16.2hh (66 in.). It may be any solid color but is usually bay, brown, or chestnut. Strong and tough, with long legs, these horses have free-striding, active action, great stamina, and are willing workers.

Racing sulkies

French Trotters are generally raced in harness. The light, two-wheeled vehicles they pull are called sulkies. They are also raced under saddle. Some French Trotters are used for general riding and for breeding riding horses. They are good jumpers.

Camargue

The Camargue region of the Rhône delta in France is a bleak and windy area. Here, the wild Camargue horses have lived on poor grazing for thousands of years. Some are tamed and ridden by local cowboys to round up wild black bulls.

Wild white horses

Camargue ponies have been called the "wild white horses of the sea." They are small at 14hh (55 in.), very tough, and always white or gray in color. They look like the horses in ancient cave paintings.

Przewalski's Horse

In the late 1870s a Russian explorer named Nicolai Przewalski discovered a herd of pony-sized wild horses in the mountains of Mongolia, on the edge of the Gobi Desert. They looked similar to the primitive herds that once roamed Asia and became known as Przewalski's Horse. Also called the Mongolian or Asiatic Wild Horse, Przewalski's Horse and the Tarpan are two surviving strains of four types of primitive horses that existed 10,000 years ago.

The breed saved
Przewalski's Horse is now extinct in the wild, but it is preserved in zoos and private studs.

Stone Age horse

Between 16,000 and 27,000 years ago early humans painted animals on the walls of caves. Some of the pictures were of horses that looked like the animal we call Przewalski's Horse. Amazingly, this breed has hardly changed at all over this long period of time.

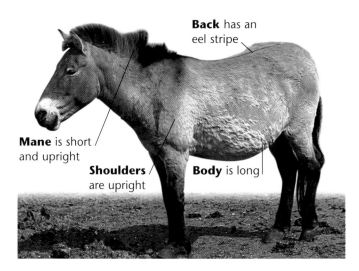

Back has an eel stripe

Mane is short and upright

Shoulders are upright

Body is long

Key facts

Przewalski's Horse	Tarpan
• **Height** 12–14.2hh (48–57 in.)	• **Height** Around 13hh (52 in.)
• **Color** Yellow dun, with black points	• **Color** Mouse dun, brown

Przewalski's Horse has similar features to primitive horses. The body is dun and has black points, and the legs may have zebra stripes. On the back is a black line called an eel stripe. The mane grows upright, and there is little or no forelock. The muzzle and the areas around the eyes are pale in color.

Face-to-face
Przewalski's Horses have large, plain heads with a convex or straight profile. Their eyes are set high up, so their heads look long.

Tarpan

The Tarpan originally lived in Russia and in Central and Eastern Europe. The breed was domesticated, but in the 1800s it became extinct. In the 1930s a Polish professor named Vetulani found ponies living in Polish forests that were like the ancient breed. With careful breeding, he recreated the Tarpan.

Quarters slope steeply

Neck is short and thick

Head is large and Roman-nosed

Body is deep

Legs have zebra stripes

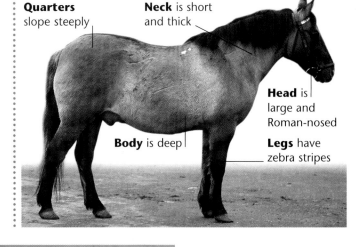

Modern Tarpan

The new breed of Tarpan lives a natural life in herds on reserves owned by the Polish government. Despite its ancient ancestry, it is much less primitive-looking than Przewalski's Horse. Although its head is quite big and its neck is quite short, the Tarpan looks much more like a modern riding pony.

Although the original Tarpan is extinct, Professor Vetulani's new breed is so similar to the old one that some people think it still exists. Like Przewalski's Horse, it has a dorsal stripe and zebra stripes on its legs. The Tarpan's mane and tail are long.

Natural jumper

This breed is a natural jumper. Both the purebred Irish Draught and the Thoroughbred cross are often used for foxhunting. They can clear all kinds of obstacles when ridden on cross-country courses.

Irish Draught

The Irish Draught was bred in its native Ireland as an all-around horse used for riding, driving, and farmwork. This breed dates back to the 1100s, and its ancestors include European heavy breeds and the Spanish Horse. It is large and strong and capable of carrying a lot of weight.

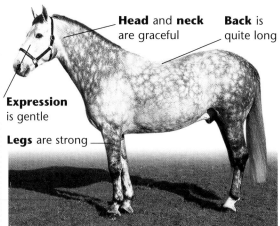

Head and **neck** are graceful

Back is quite long

Expression is gentle

Legs are strong

Despite its size—16 to 17hh (53–68 in.)—the Irish Draught is economical to keep. It has a calm temperament and is easy to ride and handle. It can be any solid color but is often gray. Although it is not very fast, this big horse is athletic and agile.

Hackney Horse

The Hackney Horse is an English breed that developed from two earlier breeds called the Norfolk Trotter and the Yorkshire Roadster. These were heavier, working horses, but the modern Hackney is more graceful because it was crossbred with Thoroughbreds. The Hackney is now a show harness horse that delights spectators with its fantastic action and appearance.

This lightly built and compact horse gives the impression of having great energy. It is high-spirited and moves very freely, throwing its forelegs well forward with each stride. Its action must be straight when seen from the front or the back.

Neck is long, graceful, and carried high

Tail is set high

Withers are low

Head is slightly Roman-nosed

Body is compact

High-stepping horse

The Hackney's action, especially when trotting, is spectacular. It raises its knees and hocks very high and, as it moves, pauses slightly on each stride, giving the impression of an effortless, floating movement.

Cleveland Bay

Quarters are powerful

Head is large and Roman-nosed

Shoulders are very strong

Body is deep and wide

Legs carry no feather

This is the oldest of the native British breeds. It has been bred in northern England since the Middle Ages. Apart from Barb and Spanish crosses in the 1600s, the breed has been kept pure. These horses are strong, hardy, long-lived, and good-natured.

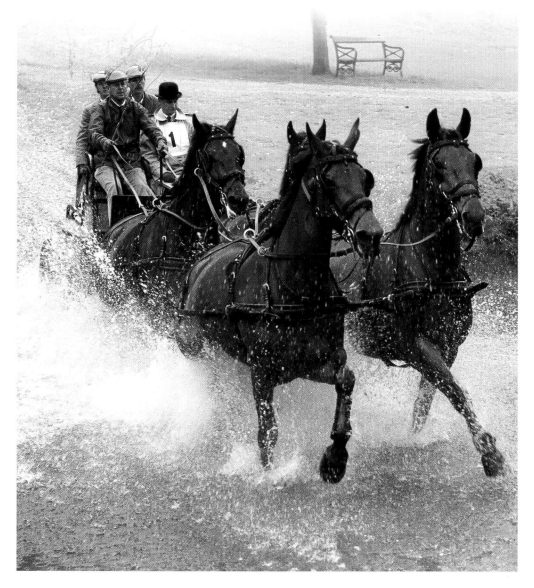

The Cleveland Bay is now classed as a rare breed. It is not used as a carriage horse so much anymore and is mainly used to cross with other breeds. As a result, the purebred Cleveland has almost disappeared.

Royal team

The Royal Mews at Buckingham Palace in London, England, has Cleveland Bays, which pull the royal carriages. The Duke of Edinburgh (left) is driving a four-in-hand team, which competes in cross-country driving events.

Key facts

• **Place of origin**
North Yorkshire, England

• **Height**
Around 16.2hh (66 in.)

• **Color**
Always bay, with no white except a star

• **Uses**
Driving, sometimes riding

Andalusian

The Andalusian horse, from southern Spain, is the modern equivalent of the ancient Spanish Horse, which influenced horse breeding worldwide. Most American breeds are descended from the Spanish Horse. The Andalucian is noble and proud, agile and athletic, with a good temperament.

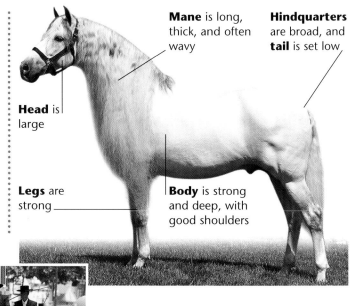

Mane is long, thick, and often wavy

Hindquarters are broad, and **tail** is set low

Head is large

Legs are strong

Body is strong and deep, with good shoulders

Ride and drive

Although it is mainly used for riding and is a popular dressage horse, the Andalusian is also driven. In its native Spain it is often used in harness during ceremonial and festive occasions.

The beautiful Andalusian horse stands between 15 and 16hh (59–64 in.). It is bay or gray in color, with the gray sometimes having a pinkish tone. The Andalusian carries itself proudly, is athletic, although not fast, and has a kind and friendly nature.

Lusitano

The Lusitano is similar to the Andalusian breed and is also descended from the Spanish Horse. It comes from Portugal and was used by the Portuguese cavalry and for light farmwork. This horse has spectacular high action, and it is taught "high school" movements. It is also used as a carriage horse.

Mane and **tail** are full, long, and often wavy

Hindquarters are sloping, and **hindlegs** are long

Profile is straight or Roman-nosed

Cannon bones are long

Back is short, and **ribs** are well-rounded

Spanish walk

This horse is performing a special "high school" movement called the Spanish walk, which it has been trained to do. In this gait the forelegs are lifted up high and stretched out in front of the horse.

The Lusitano stands between 15 and 16hh (59–64 in.), and it can be any solid color. Gray is the most common color, but this horse may also be bay, dun, chestnut, or black. The Lusitano has a short, arched neck, sloping quarters, and a compact body.

Lipizzaner

The Lipizzaner is the horse used by the famous Spanish Riding School of Vienna, Austria. It is descended from the ancient Spanish breed, which is how the school got its name. The word "Lipizzaner" comes from Lipica, Slovenia, where these horses were originally bred.

From black to gray
Lipizzaner foals are born black, and their coats gradually get lighter in color as they grow older. They may be seven years old or even older before they turn gray.

Stocky horse

The Lipizzaner is stockily built, with short, strong legs. The shape of this horse's shoulders makes it suitable for use in harness, as well as for riding. Its action tends to be high, and its feet are strong. It is an extremely intelligent horse.

Spanish school

The Spanish Riding School trains Lipizzaner stallions to perform "high school" movements in an 18th-century arena lit by large chandeliers. It takes many years to train both the horses and their riders.

Key facts

- **Place of origin**
  Lipica, Slovenia

- **Height**
  15.1–16.2hh
  (60–66 in.)

- **Color**
  Usually gray but sometimes bay

- **Uses**
  General riding and as a carriage horse

- **Characteristics**
  Intelligent, docile, and long-lived

Levade
The levade is a classical "high school" movement. The horse rears up and balances on its hind legs.

Hindquarters are powerful

Head is often Roman-nosed

Body is long and **withers** low

Neck is short and thick

Legs are powerful

Morgan

The Morgan comes from the eastern states of Massachusetts and Vermont. Morgans are descended from a stallion born in 1789, called Justin Morgan after its owner. This horse worked on the farm and raced, both in harness and under saddle.

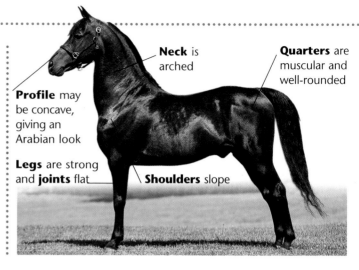

Neck is arched

Quarters are muscular and well-rounded

Profile may be concave, giving an Arabian look

Legs are strong and **joints** flat

Shoulders slope

Specially shod

Morgans are shown in either Park or Pleasure classes. Horses shown in Park classes have their feet trimmed and shod to produce a high action. If this is not done, the action is normal.

Standing between 14.2 and 15.2hh (57–61 in.), the Morgan is bay, brown, chestnut, or black in color. It is spirited, intelligent, and alert but has a good temperament and is easy to handle. Hardy, strong, and full of stamina, it is both ridden and driven.

Criollo

Descended from Spanish horses brought to South America in the 1500s, the Criollo is considered to be the toughest and soundest breed of horse in the world. The breed is native to the grassy plains of Argentina, where it is used by the gauchos, or cowboys, to work cattle. The Criollo is also found in Brazil, Uruguay, Chile, Peru, and Venezuela.

The Criollo can survive on little food in harsh climates. It is long-lived and has great stamina. In the 1920s Professor Aimé Tschiffely rode two Criollo ponies, called Mancha and Gato, from Buenos Aires, Argentina, to New York. The total distance was 9,920 mi. (16,000km).

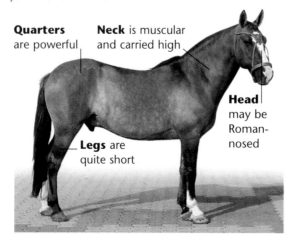

Quarters are powerful

Neck is muscular and carried high

Head may be Roman-nosed

Legs are quite short

Polo pony

Criollos are 14 to 15hh (55–59 in.) and are usually dun in color, with dark points and an eel stripe. They are often crossed with Thoroughbreds to produce the famous Argentinian polo ponies.

Quarter Horse

This first "all-American" horse was bred in Virginia in the 1600s for riding and farmwork. Its speed and agility made it perfect for working cattle. The breed got its name from English settlers who used to race these horses over quarter-mile (402m) tracks.

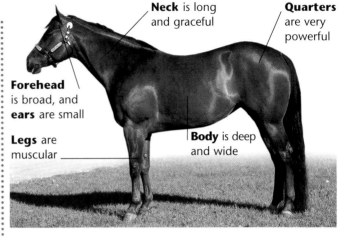

Neck is long and graceful

Quarters are very powerful

Forehead is broad, and **ears** are small

Body is deep and wide

Legs are muscular

Key facts

- **Place of origin**
  Virginia

- **Height**
  15–16hh (59–64 in.)

- **Color**
  Any solid color

- **Uses**
  Working cattle, showing

It has been claimed that the Quarter Horse is the most popular horse in the world, with over three million registered in the U.S. Agile and athletic, yet with a calm temperament, it is an ideal riding horse, as well as being superb at working cattle and performing in Western horse shows.

Sliding halt

A horse that works with cattle must be able to start, stop, and turn very quickly. In Western horse shows one of the most dramatic movements in reining classes is the sliding halt, where the horse stops instantly (right). Special shoes on the hind feet allow them to slide.

Pinto

The Pinto is a color type rather than a breed, although there are two Pinto breed registries in the United States. Descended from 16th-century Spanish horses, it has become popular in the U.S. Pintos can be black and white (piebald), chestnut, or brown and white (skewbald).

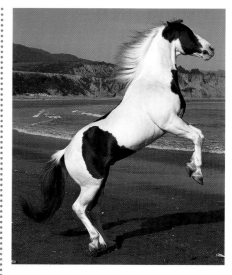

"Pinto" comes from the Spanish word *pintado*, which means "painted." There are two main color types: overo, which is mostly colored with white patches, and tobiano, which is mostly white with colored patches (rearing horse, far right). Pintos may vary in size and shape.

Mane takes the color of the neck

Foot color matches the leg

Native favorites

Pintos were favorites of the Native Americans because their coloring provided good camouflage. Today they are often bred for their color rather than their shape, and points are awarded for their markings at horse shows.

Palomino

This is another color type rather than a breed, so Palominos may be any size. The coat color should be as close as possible to that of a new gold coin, with a white mane and tail. Palominos were brought to the U.S. by the Spanish in the 1400s and 1500s.

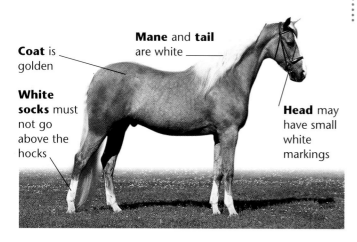

Mane and **tail** are white

Coat is golden

White socks must not go above the hocks

Head may have small white markings

Palominos are bred by crossing palomino-colored horses with chestnuts or chestnuts with creams or albinos. In 15th-century Spain the palomino color was a favorite of the powerful Queen Isabella.

Barrel racing

Palominos may be any size or type and can be used for many activities, including showing and Western classes, as well as for general riding. This horse is negotiating a tight turn at a gallop as part of a barrel race in Tampa, Florida.

Appaloosa

This breed gets its name from the Palouse River in Washington. It was bred as a workhorse by the Nez Perce tribe of Native Americans in the 1700s from imported Spanish horses. Quarter Horses have been used to improve the breed, making it a strong, compact, and good-natured horse. It is agile and athletic, has great stamina, and is a good jumper.

Eye has a white ring

Shoulders are sloping

Feet may have vertical stripes

Mane and **tail** are sparse

White over quarters is blanket marking

The main markings are leopard (white coat with dark spots—below); frost (dark background with white speckles); blanket (white quarters and loins, sometimes with dark spots); marble (roan, with a frost pattern in the center of the body and darker around the edges); and snowflake (dark background with white spots).

Key facts

- **Place of origin**
  Washington

- **Height**
  14.2–15.2hh (57–61 in.)

- **Color**
  White with dark markings

- **Uses**
  Riding, showing, jumping

Tennessee Walking Horse

This breed was developed in the 1700s and 1800s by plantation, or estate, owners in the United States, who wanted a comfortable riding horse to carry them around their large areas of land. It is called a gaited horse because it can perform three extra gaits—the flat walk, the running walk, and the rocking-chair canter. All of these movements are smooth and comfortable for the rider.

The Tennessee Walking Horse is a popular riding horse for all ages in the U.S., as well as being a show horse. The breed stands 15 to 16hh (59–61 in.) and is usually brown, bay, chestnut, or black. It is said to be the most good-tempered of all horses.

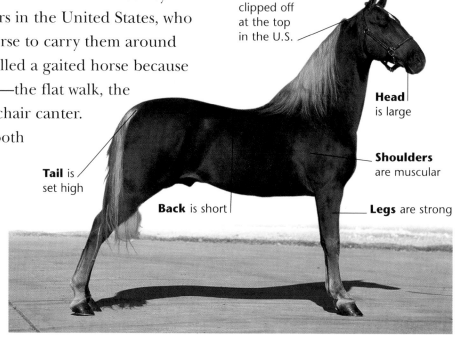

Mane is clipped off at the top in the U.S.

Head is large

Shoulders are muscular

Legs are strong

Back is short

Tail is set high

American Saddlebred

The Saddlebred was bred in Kentucky in the 1800s. It is another gaited horse—three-gaited horses perform the walk, trot, and canter with high steps; five-gaited horses also perform the slow gait and the rack, both four-beat, lateral paces. The way the horse is shod accentuates its action.

The Saddlebred is usually bay, brown, or chestnut and stands 15 to 16hh (59–64 in.). It is mostly a show horse, but if it is shod normally, it can be used for harness or general riding.

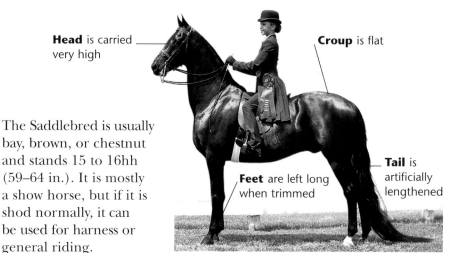

Head is carried very high

Croup is flat

Feet are left long when trimmed

Tail is artificially lengthened

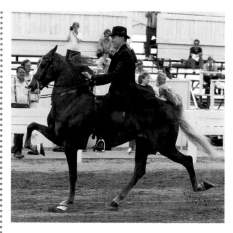

Spectacular action

The rack (above) is a fast and spectacular pace in which each leg is raised high and lands separately. Special boots protect the front heels and pasterns from being injured by the horse's hind feet as they reach far forward.

Missouri Foxtrotter

This horse was bred in the 1800s in Arkansas and Missouri as a comfortable riding horse that could cover long distances quite quickly. The breed has a unique gait called a foxtrot, in which it appears to walk with its front legs and trot with its hind legs.

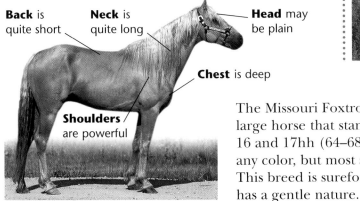

Back is quite short

Neck is quite long

Head may be plain

Chest is deep

Shoulders are powerful

The Missouri Foxtrotter is a large horse that stands between 16 and 17hh (64–68 in.). It may be any color, but most are chestnut. This breed is surefooted and has a gentle nature.

Comfortable ride

The Foxtrotter's gait is smooth and comfortable. It can travel at a speed of 5 mph (8km/h) for long distances and may go twice as fast over shorter distances. This breed is used for trail riding and showing.

Standardbred

The Standardbred is the fastest harness racing horse in the world. It was first bred in the U.S. in the 1800s. Most Standardbreds are descended from an English Thoroughbred that also had Norfolk Trotter ancestors. Standardbreds race either as trotters or pacers.

The Standardbred stands around 15.2hh (161 in.) and is usually bay, brown, or chestnut. More heavily built than the Thoroughbred, it is fast and has great stamina. This horse can cover one mile (1.6km) in one minute and 54 seconds.

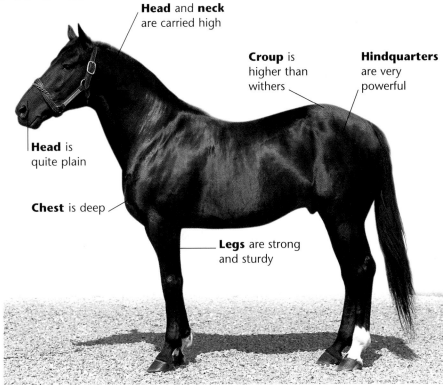

Head and **neck** are carried high

Croup is higher than withers

Hindquarters are very powerful

Head is quite plain

Chest is deep

Legs are strong and sturdy

Mustang

The tough wild horses that once roamed the plains of the western U.S. are called Mustangs. They are descended from Spanish horses taken to the U.S. in the 1500s, which were turned loose or escaped and became wild. For centuries Mustangs lived a natural life. Today special efforts are made to protect the original type of wild horse.

Mustangs range in height from 13.2 to 15hh (53–59 in.) and may be any color. They are fast, strong, agile, and hardy. They do not always have good natures, but some are domesticated and used as riding and endurance horses.

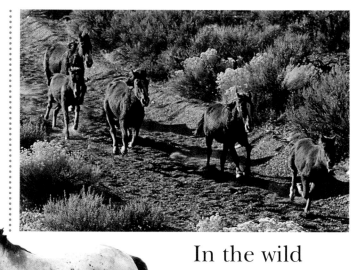

Head may be Roman-nosed

Legs are strong and tough

Body is compact

In the wild

Mustangs were rounded up and used by cowboys for cattle herding. Some were tamed and ridden by Native Americans, and others were hunted. As a result, their numbers fell, but they are now protected by U.S. laws.

Waler

The oddly named Waler is Australian—its name comes from "New South Wales." It was bred from Basuto ponies, Arabians, Barbs, and Thoroughbreds to work on the huge Australian cattle and sheep ranches. It was a cavalry horse in the Boer War and in World War I. Now it is also used for police work.

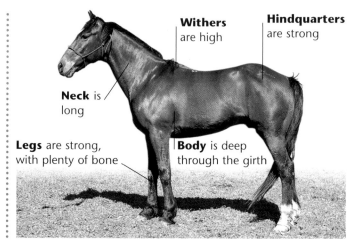

Withers are high

Hindquarters are strong

Neck is long

Legs are strong, with plenty of bone

Body is deep through the girth

Riding horse

The Waler is sometimes called the Australian Stock Horse, but it is also an ideal horse for general riding. It is fast and agile and is a natural jumper. Some Walers perform in horse shows, doing displays of buckjumping.

The Waler ranges in height from 14.2 to 16hh (57–64 in.) and may be any solid color. It is more powerfully built than the Thoroughbred. It is strong and tough, and its great powers of endurance mean that it can be ridden around ranches all day long.

Pony Breeds

Ponies are smaller than horses and have different features. They are deeper through the girth and have shorter legs. They often have feather on the lower legs and thick manes and tails. Ponies are surefooted and usually full of character.

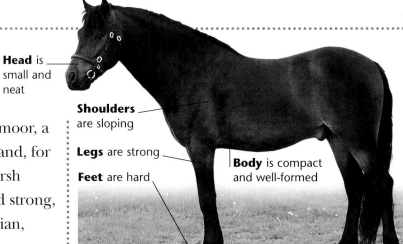

Head is small and neat

Shoulders are sloping

Legs are strong

Feet are hard

Body is compact and well-formed

Dartmoor

Small ponies have lived wild on Dartmoor, a large, rugged moor in Devon, England, for hundreds of years. Poor grazing and harsh conditions on the moors have produced strong, tough animals. Over the centuries Arabian, Thoroughbred, and Welsh Section A crosses have been used to improve this breed's quality.

The Dartmoor is a first-class children's riding pony. It is strong enough to carry a heavy weight, has good paces, jumps well, and has a good temperament. It stands around 12.2hh (50 in.) and is bay or brown in color.

Wild on the moor

There are not many purebred ponies living wild on Dartmoor today. Most of them are bred in studs. The ponies roaming the moor look quite different. In the winter, to withstand the wind, rain, and snow of their native home, they grow very thick coats and long, shaggy manes and tails.

Exmoor

This pony is from the region of southwest England known as Exmoor. It is one of the oldest breeds in the world and dates back to the last Ice Age. Today it is classed as a rare breed. It stands only 12.2 to 12.3hh (50–51 in.) but is strong enough to carry an adult.

Eye is hooded, with a light ring around it called a "toad" eye

Muzzle is light-colored

Back is broad

Tail is wide at the top

Legs are short and strong

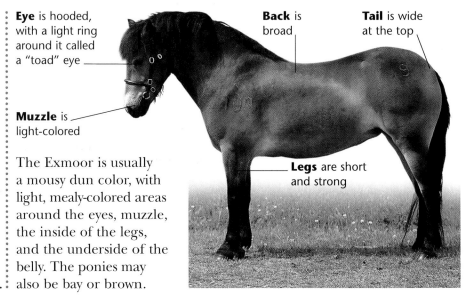

The Exmoor is usually a mousy dun color, with light, mealy-colored areas around the eyes, muzzle, the inside of the legs, and the underside of the belly. The ponies may also be bay or brown.

Connemara

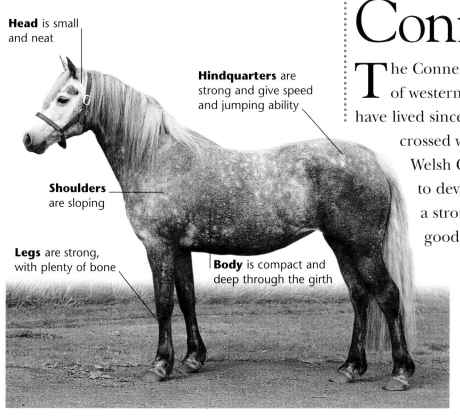

Head is small and neat

Hindquarters are strong and give speed and jumping ability

Shoulders are sloping

Legs are strong, with plenty of bone

Body is compact and deep through the girth

The Connemara comes from the moors of western Ireland, where its ancestors have lived since the 1500s. Native ponies were crossed with Spanish, Barb, Arabian, Welsh Cob, and Thoroughbred horses to develop the breed. The result was a strong, sturdy riding pony, with good paces and jumping ability.

Connemaras can be gray, dun, bay, brown, black, chestnut, or roan. They stand 13 to 14.2hh (52–57 in.) and are hardy, docile, and intelligent. They are ridden by both children and adults and make good competition horses when crossed with Thoroughbreds.

New Forest

Since the A.D. 1000s ponies have lived in the New Forest in Hampshire, England. Over the years different breeds have been introduced, including Arabians and Barbs, so New Forest ponies have a mixture of ancestors. They are fast and have good, low action.

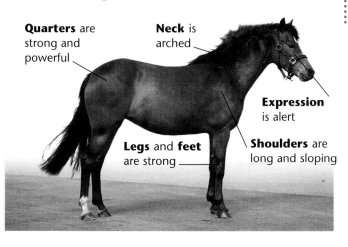

Quarters are strong and powerful

Neck is arched

Expression is alert

Legs and **feet** are strong

Shoulders are long and sloping

There are two types of ponies—one stands up to 13.1hh (53 in.) and the other 13.2 to 14.2hh (53–57 in.). Both are narrow in build, making them easy for children to ride. The ponies may be any solid color.

Forest pony

Most of the New Forest is scrubland. Local people, known as "Commoners," are allowed to keep ponies there. Many of these are in poor condition. The better examples of the breed usually come from stud farms.

Welsh Section A

The Welsh Section A, or Welsh Mountain Pony, has lived on the hills of Wales in Great Britain since pre-Roman times. It is thought to be the most beautiful pony breed. Strong and tough, with great powers of endurance, it is used for riding and driving.

Section A ponies should not stand taller than 12hh (48 in.). They look like miniature Arabians and are strong for their size. They may be any solid color, are surefooted and intelligent, and make good riding ponies.

Head is small and dished

Neck is long and graceful

Back is short and strong

Body is deep through the girth

Legs are sturdy

Welsh Section B

The Welsh Section B is also called the Welsh Pony. It was bred by crossing Section As with Section Ds and has Arabian ancestors as well. Originally the pony was used by farmers for transportation and for herding sheep that grazed on the Welsh hills. The modern type of this breed has existed since the early 1900s.

Neck is long and arched

Back is compact and strong

Head is very attractive

Legs are much longer than the Section A's

Body is deep through the girth

Section B ponies stand 12.2 to 13.2hh (50–53 in.) and may be any solid color. They have the character and gentle nature of the Section A but are more useful riding ponies because of their longer legs.

Competitive pony

As the Section B is taller than the Welsh Mountain Pony, it can be ridden by larger children and used in competitions such as gymkhana events. It has long, low action and is also a good jumper.

Welsh Section C

This pony was originally bred by crossing the Section A and Section D and is known as the Welsh Pony of Cob Type. Smaller than the Welsh Cob but stockier in build than the Welsh Pony, it was once used for all types of farmwork, as well as in the slate quarries of North Wales. Today it is often used for trekking and trail riding, as well as driving.

Neck is thick and carried high

Quarters are very muscular

Head is attractive

Shoulders are powerful

Legs are strong

This small pony should not stand taller than 13.2hh (53 in.). Despite its size, the Section C is very strong. It is also hardy enough to live outside all year long. It has a good temperament and may be any solid color.

Driving pony

With their fast action, Section C ponies are ideal for driving. They are also good riding ponies, can jump well, and are strong enough to carry light adults, as well as children.

Welsh Section D

The Section D, or Welsh Cob, was bred from the Welsh Mountain Pony, with crosses to Spanish horses, trotters, and Arabians between the 1000s and 1800s. The Cob was used for all-around farmwork and riding and for pulling carts in cities.

The Section D stands between 14.2 and 15.2hh (57–61 in.) and may be any solid color. It is famous for its fast, high-stepping trot, is an ideal driving pony, a good jumper, and is also used for riding and trekking.

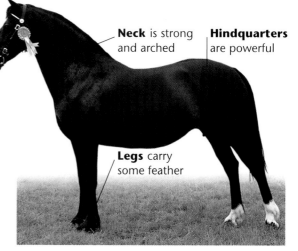

Head looks like a pony's

Neck is strong and arched

Hindquarters are powerful

Legs carry some feather

Fell

This breed of pony is around 2,000 years old. Fell ponies come from Cumbria, England, and have Friesian ancestors. They were used as pack animals to carry lead from the mines to the docks and often traveled 240 mi. (386km) in one week. They were also ridden and driven and used for farmwork and herding.

These ponies are only 14hh (55 in.), but they can carry 220 lb. (100kg) packs or be ridden by adults. They are strong, hardy, surefooted, and energetic. They are always black or dark brown, with only small white markings allowed.

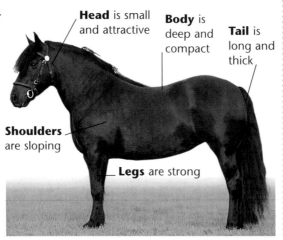

Head is small and attractive

Body is deep and compact

Tail is long and thick

Shoulders are sloping

Legs are strong

Good riding pony

The Fell's sloping shoulders make it more suitable for riding than the Dales pony, and it can be ridden by everyone in the family. It is also used for trekking. The Fell does well in harness and is popular for competition driving.

Dales

This strong and sturdy pony comes from Durham, North Yorkshire, and Northumberland, England. It was used as a pack pony to carry lead across the hills. The breed is around 2,000 years old and has Welsh Cob and Clydesdale ancestors.

The Dales is more of a harness pony than the Fell. It is taller, more solidly built, and has higher knee action. It stands around 14.2hh (57 in.) and is usually black in color. The Dales is also used for general riding.

Neck is thick and arched

Back is strong and muscular

Head looks like a pony's

Legs are short and strong and carry feather

Chest is broad and deep

Highland

The Highland has existed in Scotland since the last Ice Age and is the largest of Great Britain's pony breeds. They were bred for farmwork, forestry, and deer tracking, and there were three sizes—the smallest from the islands and the largest from the mainland. Today there is little difference between the three.

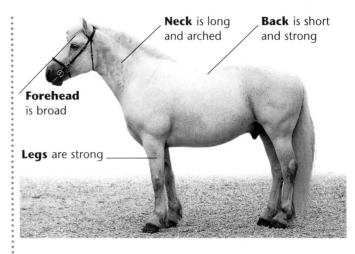

Neck is long and arched

Back is short and strong

Forehead is broad

Legs are strong

Powerfully built and very strong, the Highland looks like some of the ponies that are seen in ancient cave paintings. It often has an eel stripe along its back and zebra markings on its legs. Its shoulders are huge, and its feet are hard and tough. It is long-lived, easy to keep, and has a docile, gentle nature.

Key facts

- **Place of origin**
  Scottish Highlands, U.K.

- **Height**
  13–14.2hh (52–57 in.)

- **Color**
  Gray, dun, brown, black

- **Uses**
  Riding, trekking, harness

Champion pony
The champion Highland stallion Duart of Glenmuick (right) has the breed's characteristic full mane and tail.

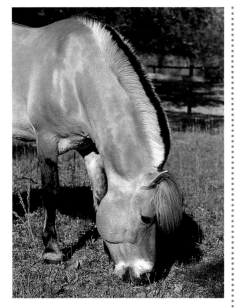

Fjord

The Fjord is an ancient breed descended from Przewalski's Horse. It has many characteristics of primitive horses, being dun in color, with a dorsal stripe and sometimes zebra stripes on its legs. The Fjord is strong and surefooted, hardy, and economical to keep and has great powers of endurance.

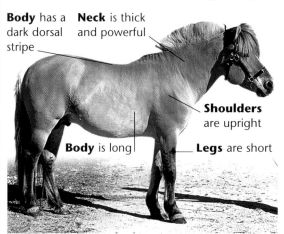

Body has a dark dorsal stripe

Neck is thick and powerful

Shoulders are upright

Body is long

Legs are short

The Vikings used ponies that looked like the Fjord and shipped them in longboats to Scotland and Iceland. Since ancient times this pony has been used for work on mountain farms, as well as being a riding and pack pony. This pony stands between 13 and 14.2hh (52–57 in.).

Special mane

The Fjord's mane is dark in the center and silvery white on the outside. It is cut to stand upright in a long curve, with the outer hair shorter than at the center.

Icelandic

Although the Icelandic is small, some people call it a horse. It stands between 12.3 and 13.2hh (51–53 in.) but is strong enough to carry an adult for long distances. The Vikings brought these ponies to Iceland, and the breed has been kept pure for 1,000 years. Icelandics are ridden, driven, and used for trekking.

Quarters slope from the croup

Shoulders are upright

Head is large

Body is long

Legs are short and strong

As well as walking, trotting, cantering, and galloping, Icelandic ponies can perform a gait called the *skeid*, which is pacing, and the *tölt*, which is a fast, running walk. They take part in competitions for gaited horses.

Outdoor pony

Although the Icelandic winter is harsh, these ponies often live outside in a semiwild state. This makes them tough and hardy. They are also very surefooted, moving easily over the rough and mountainous ground of their island home.

Haflinger

These ponies have been bred in the Austrian mountains for over 200 years. All native Haflingers have a brand mark—a letter "H" and an edelweiss, the national flower of Austria. They were used for all types of farm and forestry work, as well as for riding. They are now popular trekking ponies.

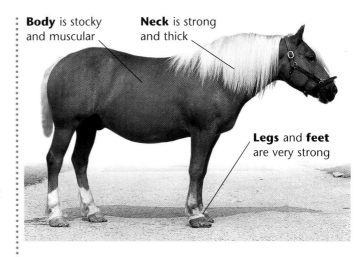

Body is stocky and muscular

Neck is strong and thick

Legs and **feet** are very strong

As well as being sturdy and tough, Haflingers usually live for a long time. They start working at four years old and may continue until the age of 40—almost twice as long as the average horse. Haflingers have a docile temperament and are easy to handle.

Key facts

- **Place of origin**
  Austrian Tyrol

- **Height**
  13.1–14.2hh (53–57 in.)

- **Color**
  Chestnut or palomino

- **Uses**
  Riding, trekking, harness

Sleigh ride
Haflingers pull sleighs in the winter. Their harnesses may be decorated for Christmas.

New breeds of the U.S.

Some stallions produce foals that have similar characteristics to their sire, or father. This quality is called prepotency, and horses that have it may be used to start new breeds. Once a breed is established, a stud book is set up in which horses that meet the breed's standards are registered.

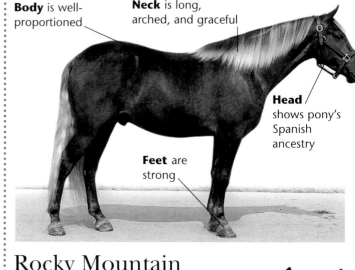

Body is well-proportioned

Neck is long, arched, and graceful

Head shows pony's Spanish ancestry

Feet are strong

Rocky Mountain

This pony may be the world's most recent breed—it was registered in the stud book in 1986. Although there are other colors, the favorite is a unique chocolate brown, with a flaxen mane and tail. The Rocky Mountain is sometimes called a horse because of its height. It is hardy and can survive in harsh winter weather.

Ears are exceptionally long

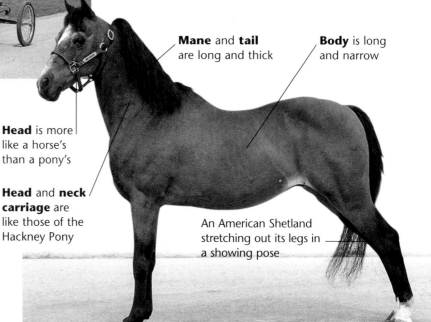

Show driving
An American Shetland driving a show carriage is a popular attraction in the U.S. This pony also races in harness, and some types are ridden and jumped in the showring.

American Shetland

This pony is very different from the Shetland of the British Isles. The breed was developed in the 1880s by crossing lightly built Shetlands with Hackney ponies, and the result was a Hackney-type show harness pony.

Head is more like a horse's than a pony's

Head and **neck carriage** are like those of the Hackney Pony

Mane and **tail** are long and thick

Body is long and narrow

An American Shetland stretching out its legs in a showing pose

Special gait

Although this graceful animal is cantering, the characteristic action of the Rocky Mountain is a natural ambling four-beat gait. The Rocky Mountain can reach speeds of up to 20 mph.

Key facts

Rocky Mountain

- **Height**
  14.2–15hh (57–59 in.)

- **Color**
  Chocolate, with flaxen mane and tail, plus others

American Shetland

- **Height**
  Up to 11.2hh (46 in.)

- **Color**
  Any solid color

Pony of the Americas

- **Height**
  11.2–13hh (46–52 in.)

- **Color**
  Markings are the same as the Appaloosa

Pony of the Americas

This breed was started in Iowa in the 1950s when a Shetland was crossed with an Appaloosa. The foal that they produced was the first of the breed. Ponies of the Americas are small and stocky and have traditional Appaloosa markings. These ponies are docile and good-natured.

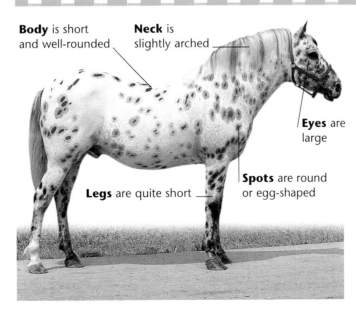

Body is short and well-rounded

Neck is slightly arched

Eyes are large

Spots are round or egg-shaped

Legs are quite short

On the leading rein

These ponies are small and easy to handle, so they are good for children who are learning to ride. First lessons are often on a leading rein.

Caspian

The Caspian is possibly the oldest breed of horse or pony that exists, and it may be the ancestor of the Arabian. Since prehistoric times it has lived near the southern coast of the Caspian Sea in what is now Iran. In the mid-1900s the breed was rediscovered, and these ponies are now bred in Europe, North America, Australia, and New Zealand.

The Caspian looks more like a miniature horse than a pony. It is lightly built, has a fine, silky coat, mane, and tail, and is very fast for its size. The Caspian stands 10 to 12hh (40–48 in.), and it is usually bay or chestnut in color.

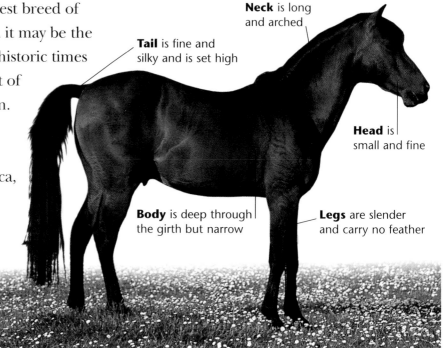

Neck is long and arched

Tail is fine and silky and is set high

Head is small and fine

Body is deep through the girth but narrow

Legs are slender and carry no feather

Chincoteague and Assateague

Chincoteague and Assateague are islands off the coast of Virginia, where these small wild ponies have lived since the 1500s. They may be the descendants of Barb horses that were once shipwrecked there.

Quarters slope sharply from the croup

Back is short

Head may be large and plain

These ponies have lived on islands for hundreds of years so they have not been crossed with other breeds. They stand around 12hh (148 in.) and may be any color. They are often skewbald or piebald (see Pinto on page 42).

Island ponies

Once a year the Assateague ponies are taken across to Chincoteague island, where the young animals are sold. These ponies are strong-willed and may be difficult to handle, but some are used for riding.

Basuto

This pony is named after the area of South Africa where it was developed between the 1600s and 1800s. It has Arabian, Barb, and Thoroughbred ancestors. The Basuto often had to endure harsh conditions, so this breed is strong and tough. The British used Basuto ponies during the Boer War.

The Basuto stands around 14.2hh (57 in.). It has great stamina and can be ridden every day for many miles. This makes the Basuto a popular trekking pony. It is usually brown, bay, chestnut, or gray in color.

Head may have Arabian features

Neck is thin

Back is long

Shoulders are upright

Feet are hard

Herding pony

Farmers in Lesotho, South Africa, use Basuto ponies for herding animals, as well as for riding around their land. In the past these ponies have been raced and were also used by the army and for polo. They are popular general riding ponies in southern Africa.

Boer

The Boer pony developed in the 1800s in South Africa and has similar ancestors to the Basuto. Most Boer ponies did not have to endure such harsh conditions as the Basuto, so this breed is often taller and of better quality. The Boer is known as the "Boerperd" in its native country. It is found in the northeastern part of South Africa, where it is used as an all-around farm horse.

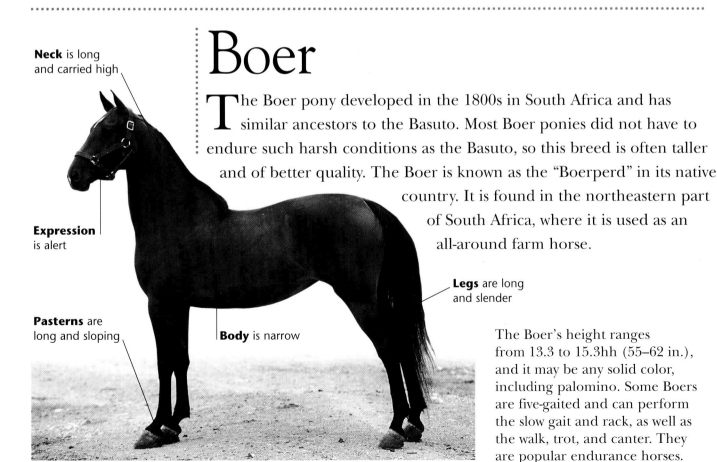

Neck is long and carried high

Expression is alert

Pasterns are long and sloping

Body is narrow

Legs are long and slender

The Boer's height ranges from 13.3 to 15.3hh (55–62 in.), and it may be any solid color, including palomino. Some Boers are five-gaited and can perform the slow gait and rack, as well as the walk, trot, and canter. They are popular endurance horses.

Australian

Ponies were first brought to Australia in the early 1800s, and in the 1900s the Australian pony officially became a breed. Its ancestors include the Hackney Pony, the Shetland, the Arabian, the Thoroughbred, and the Welsh Mountain Pony (Section A), which it closely resembles.

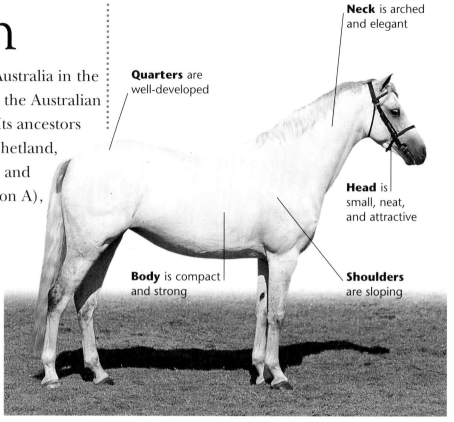

Quarters are well-developed

Neck is arched and elegant

Head is small, neat, and attractive

Body is compact and strong

Shoulders are sloping

The Australian pony stands between 12 and 14hh (48–55 in.) and is an attractive animal. Its action is free and level, and it is good-natured and easy to handle. This breed may be any solid color, and in Australia it is a popular riding and show pony.

Falabella

The little Falabella is named after the family who created it near Buenos Aires, Argentina, in the early 1900s. They crossed tiny Shetland ponies with a small Thoroughbred and kept breeding using the smallest ponies produced. Falabellas are inbred, so they are not strong and need a lot of care and attention. They are not ridden, although they are sometimes driven. Falabellas are mostly kept as pets.

Tiny foal

Falabella foals stand only around 4hh (16 in.), but they grow quickly. When the mother is pregnant, she carries her foal for 13 months, which is two months longer than other horses and ponies.

Tail is set low

Legs are not very strong

Body is deep

Mane and **tail** are thick

Head is large

Falabellas stand around 7 to 8.2hh (28–34 in.) and may be any color. People think of them as miniature horses rather than small ponies because they have fine bones and slender legs. They are clever and friendly and make good pets.

Shetland

The Shetland is the smallest of Great Britain's mountain and moorland ponies. It has lived in the bleak Shetland Islands, northeast of Scotland, for around 10,000 years. The harsh climate and poor grazing have made it very hardy. For its size the Shetland is probably the strongest of all horses and ponies.

Body is deep and compact

Head is neat

Tail is full

Legs are short

Shetlands are measured in inches, not in hands, and are up to 42 in. (107cm) high. They can be any color. They are used as children's riding ponies and in harness, where they are especially good at scurry driving.

Tough ponies

These ponies can survive in the snow and strong winds of their island home. They grow thick coats and can live on very little food. Their small size means they can find shelter more easily than larger ponies.

Hackney Pony

The Hackney Pony is a smaller, ponylike version of the Hackney Horse. It was produced in the 1800s from Fell and Welsh ponies and the Yorkshire Trotter. These early ponies were very hardy, and today's Hackneys are strong and tough, with great stamina. Hackneys have a high neck carriage, short, compact bodies, and long, powerful legs. They can be 12.2 to 14hh (50–55 in.) and are brown, bay, or black.

Spectacular action

The Hackney's high-stepping action is a spectacular sight and produces much applause in the showring. Around 100 years ago these ponies could be seen on city streets, where they were used by tradesmen delivering goods. Today they are almost always show harness ponies.

Glossary

Appaloosa

Oldenburg

You may not understand all the words you come across as you read about horses and ponies and learn more about their world. This list explains what some of the words mean.

acquired mark A mark on a horse's or pony's body that is the result of an injury.

action The way that a horse or pony moves. "High action" means that the legs are lifted high off the ground, and "low action" means that they are kept close to the ground.

blaze A white mark down the front of a horse's face.

bone The measurement around the **cannon bone** just below the knee. "**Plenty of bone**" means a high measurement and therefore strong legs.

brand mark A mark that is burned into a horse's skin with a hot iron. Brand marks show that an animal belongs to a certain breed or ranch.

breed association An organization that regulates the breeding of its particular breed of horse or pony.

buckjumping Leaping in the air with all four feet at once and the back arched.

cannon bone The bone in the foreleg between the **knee** and the **fetlock**.

clean-legged Legs that carry no **feather**.

coat The hair covering an animal's skin.

cob A short-legged, stocky riding horse.

competition horse A horse that takes part in competitions, usually reining, eventing, dressage, or show jumping.

conformation The overall shape and proportions of a horse or pony.

crest The center of the arch on the **top line** of the neck.

cross-country A riding course with jumps that must be completed within a specified time. Cross-country is part of **eventing.**

croup The highest point of the hindquarters.

deep through the girth Deep and broad through the chest and behind the **elbows**. This gives a lot of space for the heart and lungs.

diagonal When a horse trots, its legs move in diagonal pairs. This means that the right **hind leg** and left **foreleg** move at the same time.

dished face A face that is concave, or curving inward, in profile, like the Arabian's.

docile Quiet and calm.

dock The top of a horse's tail.

dorsal stripe A line that runs along the back—see **eel stripe**.

draft horse A big, heavy horse used for pulling loads or farm implements.

dressage The advanced schooling and training of a horse, performed in competitions.

driving A horse that is driven is being used to pull a carriage.

eel stripe A dark stripe along a horse's or pony's back from its mane to its tail.

elbow The joint at the top of the **foreleg**.

endurance riding A long-distance riding competition.

eventing A competition made up of **dressage, cross-country,** and **show jumping**.

feather The long hair that grows on the lower part of the legs of most heavy horses and some ponies.

fetlock The joint on the lower part of a horse's leg just above the foot.

forearm The upper part of the **foreleg**.

foreleg The front leg.

forelock The part of a horse's or pony's mane that falls over the forehead.

four-beat pace One in which each foot hits the ground separately such as the walk.

four-in-hand A team of four driving horses, with two in front and two behind.

gait The **pace** at which a horse or pony moves. The four natural gaits are walk, trot, canter, and gallop.

gaited An American term describing a horse that can perform more gaits than the natural ones. Horses may be three-gaited or five-gaited.

girth a) The part of a horse where the saddle's girth fits just behind the **forelegs**. b) The broad strap that holds the saddle in place.

gymkhana Games and races on horseback; an event usually held as part of a show.

hand A horse's or pony's height is measured in hands. One hand equals 4 in. (10cm).

harness The equipment used on a horse that is being driven. "**In harness**" means being driven.

hh The abbreviation for "hands." Stands for "hands high."

hind leg The back leg.

hindquarters The rump.

hock The joint halfway down the **hind leg**.

Shire

Welsh ponies

Solid color

Pinto

Thoroughbreds

hunter A horse used for foxhunting. It must be able to gallop and jump well.

inbred Bred from animals that are closely related to each other.

in hand Leading a horse or pony while on foot.

in harness *see* **harness**.

knee The joint halfway down the **foreleg**.

lateral At the side. A lateral **pace** is when both legs on the same side move together.

living out Living in a field rather than a stable.

markings, record of A horse's or pony's markings are recorded on vaccination certificates and passports.

mealy Light-colored or the color of oatmeal.

Norfolk Trotter A fast-trotting harness horse that existed between the 1400s and mid-1900s; ancestor of the Hackney and others.

pace a) Another word for **gait**. b) A gait in which both legs on the same side of a horse move together.

pack pony A pony that carries heavy loads in packs that are strapped to its back.

partbred A horse or pony that has one **purebred** parent or two purebred parents of different breeds.

part-colored When a horse is more than one color such as skewbald.

pastern The part of the horse's leg between the **fetlock** and the foot.

pedigree A table that lists an animal's parents, grandparents, great-grandparents, etc.

plain head An unattractive or ugly head.

point of the shoulder The front of the shoulder joint where the shoulder blade joins the first bone of the animal's **foreleg**.

points a) The physical features of a horse. b) The parts of a bay or dun horse that are black (the mane, tail, and lower legs).

ponylike head A small, neat head with small ears and large eyes.

presence The way that a horse or pony carries itself.

primitive When it is used to describe a breed, "primitive" means at an early stage of evolution.

purebred A horse or pony that has two parents of the same breed **registered** in the breed's **stud book**.

quarters Another word for **hindquarters**.

rack A fast **pace** in which each foot hits the ground separately.

registered Listed in the **stud book** of the breed to which the horse or pony belongs.

roaching Cutting off a horse's or pony's mane.

Roman nose A nose that, seen in profile, is convex, or curving outward.

scurry driving A speed driving competition that uses small ponies in pairs.

showing Exhibiting a horse or pony at a horse show, where it is judged on its **conformation** and **paces**.

show jumping A jumping competition at a horse show.

sloping shoulders Shoulders that slope from the **withers** to the **point of the shoulder**. They give smooth, comfortable **paces** in a riding horse.

slow gait A slow, **four-beat**, high-stepping **gait**.

solid color The same color all over, with markings only on the legs and face.

sound A "sound" horse is a healthy one, with no lameness or breathing problems.

Spanish Horse The most important European breed of horse for centuries, which had a huge impact on horse breeding throughout the world. Most American breeds are descended from the Spanish Horse.

stamina The ability to keep going even when very tired.

straight action Moving the legs straight forward and backward without any sideways movement.

straight shoulders *see* **upright shoulders**.

stud book A book in which the name, date of birth, and **pedigree** of a **purebred** horse or pony is **registered**, or listed. Every horse and pony breed has a stud book.

stud farm A place where horses or ponies are bred. These are also referred to as "studs."

temperament A horse's or pony's nature, for example, calm, gentle, or excitable.

top line The upper part of a horse's back from the **withers** to the **hindquarters**.

trot A **diagonal pace** in which the feet hit the ground in pairs.

under saddle When a horse or pony is ridden.

up to weight Capable of carrying a heavy rider.

upright shoulders Shoulders that do not slope very much from the **withers** to the **point of the shoulder**. They are better for carrying a **harness** collar.

withers The bony ridge at the base of a horse's neck.

zebra marks Horizontal dark stripes on the legs of **primitive** breeds of ponies.

Index

HORSE AND PONY WEB SITES
www.equestrian.org
(American Horse Shows
Association—U.S.A. Equestrian)
www.haynet.net
(a comprehensive directory
of horse-related web sites)
www.horsesport.org
(International Federation
of Equestrian Sport)
www.ilph.org
(International League for
the Protection of Horses)
www.imh.org
(The International Museum
of the Horse)
www.ponyclub.org
(official U.S. Pony Clubs web site)
www.youngrider.com
(links to other horse and pony
web sites)

ford, Sandy

& pony breed